How to Cross a Pond

poems about water

by **Marilyn Singer**

illustrated by **Meilo So**

Alfred A. Knopf
New York

In Memory of My Good Friend Easy,
Who Loved to Cross a Pond

Many thanks to Steve Aronson, David Lubar,
Dian Curtis Regan, my wonderful editor Janet Schulman,
and the gang at Random House.

THIS IS A BORZOI BOOK PUBLISHED BY ALFRED A. KNOPF

Text copyright © 2003 by Marilyn Singer
Illustrations copyright © 2003 by Meilo So

www.randomhouse.com/kids

Library of Congress Cataloging-in-Publication Data
Singer, Marilyn
How to cross a pond : poems about water / by Marilyn Singer ;
illustrated by Meilo So.—1st ed.
p.   cm.
Summary: Such poems as "Babbling Brook," "Spring in the Garden,"
"Watercolors," "City River," and "Ocean Checklist"
present some of the many facets of water.
ISBN 0-375-82376-X (trade) — ISBN 0-375-92376-4 (lib. bdg.)
1. Water—Juvenile poetry. 2. Children's poetry, American.
[1. Water—Poetry. 2. American poetry.] I. So, Meilo, ill. II. Title.
PS3569.I546 H69 2003
811'.54—dc21   2002034210

Printed in the United States of America

August 2003

10   9   8   7   6   5   4   3   2   1

First Edition

Contents

Water Music

Water has such a powerful voice
It speaks to ducks and bears and seals
   To salamanders, dragonflies
      albatrosses, eels
To waders, swimmers, sailors, skippers
      of rowboats, schooners, liners, clippers
Water hums lullabies of home
      sings ballads of journeys great and small
Even when it whispers
         we hear water's call
      and answer with need, in hope, by choice
            Water has such a powerful voice

Babbling Brook

The brook it really babbles
       It murmurs and it mutters
It's lively and it's sleepy
       It's eloquent, it stutters
What's it telling? What's it saying?
       Is it grave or is it playing?
If my ears were only sharper
       If my tongue a bit less bookish
It would be grand to understand
            and speak with it in Brookish

7

Dress-Up

Each morning in the garden I watch the daily game
of dress-up.
Diamond necklaces of dew or lace collars of frost,
Feathered hats of snow or tiaras of ice.
Water is so excellent a designer—
each fashion unique
and guaranteed to change with every season,
so no tree is ever caught
in yesterday's old clothes.

How to Cross a Pond

You can swim
> or you can float
on a raft
> or in a boat.

You can skate
> and you can row.
You can get
> your dog to tow.

You can fly
> if you're a hawk.
And in the winter
> you can walk.

Lost and Found

When the snow melts
     my street becomes a lost-and-found.
There are my mother's earrings, my sister's ball,
     the test I nearly passed, the homework I really lost.
Here are the stoopsitters, hoopshooters, ropejumpers,
     the neighbors I haven't seen since the blizzard came.
Everywhere are the fuzzy buds and tufts of grass,
     the pale shoots and sprouts missing since last March.
When the snow melts
     my street loses its tired, wet winter coat
and finds again its shiny new spring shoes.

Spring in the Garden

In the lotus pool
      koi swim; Heron perches
on the No Fishing sign.

In the lotus pool
      Duck floats; two drakes argue
about who saw her first.

Fair-Weather Friend

I'm a fair-weather friend to the rain.
A week of it in April and I complain.
No talk of tulips or daisies
        will cancel my crazies.
I've no use for that showers-and-flowers refrain.

But soon, day after midsummer day,
When the sky never seems to turn gray,
I'm so tired of the haze
        and the sun's steady blaze,
I wish the rain would remember to come down
        and play!

Watercolors

Turquoise, teal, aquamarine,
Silver, charcoal, smoke,
      these are the colors of water
we see in sunlight, in rain.
Brown, too, of mud and cattails,
Red of clay,
Yellow of fallen leaves.
And then there's black.
Not the velvet dark at nighttime
      but the deep down fathomless dark
where fish, all teeth and throat,
      drift, glowing by their own light,
or swim sightless in sunless caves far underground.
The black of sleep
      as thorough as only water can allow.
The black we'd have to see
      not to see,
to understand just how black

                    black can be.

Rain Forest

In the rain forest, where the ground is a limitless
sponge
drinking in cloud after cloud's worth
of water,
the treetops are ablaze with private ponds
each no bigger than a flower's cup.
Tadpoles hatch within them
swimming leisurely
turning into tiny frogs,
each one master of its estate
where every petal is a teeming shore
every pool a boundless lake.

Underwater Ballet

Flower petals
Pumpkinseeds
       Dozing catfish
       Fallen reeds
Tiny feathers
Silver floats
       Dangling goggles
       Little boats
Diving beetles
Dark gray rocks
       Rainbow bubbles
       Drifting socks
Flashing elbows
Sunken logs
       Knobby kneecaps
       Leaping frogs
Trailing fingers
Plumes of spray
       Flapping flippers
         Pond ballet

23

Oasis

If a pond is an oasis
      in the desert
a blessing of palms
      to perching birds
      and travelers grown weary of sand,
Is an island an oasis
      in the ocean?
A gift of palms
      to perching birds
      and travelers grown weary of water
         sailors hungry for a taste of land?

25

Frog Prince

Down under the wet
        green
my brother dreams
    of a life amphibious.
To swim for hours
    without surfacing,
To breathe through damp
      skin.
In his closet a tangle
    of snorkels, fins,
      goggles and slippery suits
tells the story of so many brave failures:
    No matter how hard he tries
      this prince will never be
        a frog.

27

Water Guns

We're having a water war
    A spurt and squirty
     clean but dirty
    I'm-gonna-find-you
    Look-out-behind-you
        water war
You zap my elbow
    I whap your knee
It's a stalk and a race
    Who will score in the face?
We're all wet
    and we'll get wetter
We've got water on the brain
We're feeling good
    and we'll feel better—
And then it starts
    to rain

29

City River

Who could believe our sudden summer stream
our splay and spray
just today
waterway
the stubby hydrant brings
is the same wild river that springs
from the melting mountains far away
where hemlocks sway
brook trout stay
otters play
each winter day

31

Wells

Water is too easy here,
                grandma says.
Taps and toilets,
        hoses and hydrants,
A quick twist, swish, run.
To appreciate water
                you must work for it,
Pump, hoist, and haul.
Learn to love
                the heft of the bucket
                        in your hands,
                the weight of the cool jar
                        on your head.
Learn to understand
                that water is the true treasure
                        of small villages and great cities.
Only then will you never squander
        what is not yours to own.

33

The Moon's Gravity

I feel sorry for the moon
      the dry moon
tugging at the earth's oceans
      as if she could draw them up
          to fill her vast dusty seas
Even Mars
      distant Mars
 it seems has real water
      where tiny creatures may perhaps lie

                                 multiply

      under a layer of rock
But the moon
      the poor moon
must make do with memories
      of tall, two-legged visitors
who stopped briefly by years ago
      then returned to their blue planet
to gaze at her tearless face
      and feel her dragging the waves
         from under their sandy feet

What Water Can Be

A furrow that's filling
        Water, collective
Your face in the puddle
        Water, reflective
A network of rivers
        Water, connective
Your boat drifting downstream
        Water, directive
A storm in the city
        Water, objective
One drop on your eyelash
        Water, selective

Meandering

Something in water loves

the curve

the bend

the zigzag

the swerve.

Water will never be the type

to prefer the ditch

the canal

the pipe.

Rain running down

a windowpane

or river rushing

through a state,

water chooses

crooked.

It doesn't care for

straight.

Something in water finds it grander

to be commander

of meander.

Ocean Checklist

Vast, blue-green or winter gray.

Tastes like salt, sends up spray.

Feeds its fishes, also whales.

Knows of breezes, also gales.

Changes tides and rolls out waves.

Sometimes sings and sometimes raves.

Welcomes ships at work or leisure—

Swallows some and hoards their treasure.

Likes to give and likes to keep.

Is everybody's dream of deep.